God Loves

Aardvarks

And God Loves Me

An Acrostic Devotional By
PAMELA A. TAYLOR
with Heather Hart

My Father | Copyright © 2000, 2020 by Pam Taylor
ISBN | 978-1-7351646-5-6

Cover Design & Book Layout by Heather Hart
Cross Graphic © Clker-Free-Vector-Images | Pixabay
Aardvark Graphic © Nina Piankova | DepositPhotos.com

The author of this book can be contacted for
permissions, additional copies, and speaking inquiries at:
LoavesandFishesCoaching.com

"Looking forward to that wonderful time we've been expecting, when his glory shall be seen—the glory of our great God and Savior Jesus Christ. He died under God's judgment against our sins so that he could rescue us from constant falling into sin and make us his very own people, with cleansed hearts and real enthusiasm for doing kind things for others."
Titus 2:13-14

With Huge Gratitude...

To the Creator of Aardvarks

Dedicated...

Put Your Name Here: _____

A

GOD, THANK YOU FOR AARDVARKS.

The Bible says...

"...For I am convinced that nothing can ever separate us from his love. Death can't, and life can't. The angels won't, and all the powers of hell itself cannot keep God's love away. Our fears for today, our worries about tomorrow, [39] or where we are—high above the sky, or in the deepest ocean—nothing will ever be able to separate us from the love of God demonstrated by our Lord Jesus Christ when he died for us."
Romans 8:38-39

Thank You, God, that you love funny looking Aardvarks, animals, bugs, and things. And thank you, God, that you love me, even when kids make fun of my big ears.

Thank You.

Draw Your Prayer

B

God, Thank You For Letting Me Believe in You

The Bible says…

"Now we believe because we have heard him ourselves,
not just because of what you told us. He is indeed the
Savior of the world."
Mathew 18:6

Thank you, God, that I believe you when you say you love
me, no matter how many times I mess up.

Thank You.

Draw Your Prayer

C

GOD, THANK YOU FOR CARING ABOUT ME.

The Bible says…

"Let him have all your worries and cares, for he is always thinking about you and watching everything that concerns you."
1 Peter 5:7

Like Samuel in the Bible, thank you, God, that you speak to me whenever I take the time to listen.

Thank You.

Draw Your Prayer

D

GOD, THANK YOU FOR DINOSAURS.

The Bible says…

"Remember, I commanded you to be strong and brave.
Don't be afraid, because the Lord your God will be with
you wherever you go."
Joshua 1:9, ERV

Thank you, God, that dinosaurs are extinct.
They're scary and big.

Thank You.

Draw Your Prayer

E

God, Thank You For Loving Everybody.

The Bible says…

""I see very clearly that the Jews are not God's only favorites! In every nation he has those who worship him and do good deeds and are acceptable to him."
Acts 10:34-35

Thank you, God, you don't only love certain kinds or colors of people. You love everybody, and you love us all the time.

Thank You.

Draw Your Prayer

F

God, Thank You That You Are Fair.

The Bible says…

"Now, in Christ, it doesn't matter if you are a Jew or a Greek, a slave or free, male or female. You are all the same in Christ Jesus."
Galatians 3:28, ERV

Thank you, God, that you don't play favorites. You treat everybody just the same. Whew! I'm glad about that because sometimes kids and even grown-ups have favorites.

Thank You.

Draw Your Prayer

G

GOD, THANK YOU THAT YOU GET ME.

The Bible says...

"O Lord, you have examined my heart and know
everything about me."
Psalm 139:1

Thank you, God, that you "get" me. Even when I don't
"get" myself. Why do I do foolish things?

Thank You.

Draw Your Prayer

H

GOD, THANK YOU FOR GIVING ME HOPE.

The Bible says…

"But they that wait upon the Lord shall renew their strength. They shall mount up with wings like eagles; they shall run and not be weary; they shall walk and not faint."
Isaiah 40:31

God, thank you for hope. Grown-ups talk about it all the time. I know hope is good, but what is hope? And why is it good?

Thank You.

Draw Your Prayer

I

GOD, THANK YOU FOR YOUR INTEREST IN ME.

The Bible says…

"You know where I go and where I lie down.
You know everything I do."
Psalm 139:3, ERV

Thank you, God, that you're interested in me, just
because I'm me. You never get tired of hearing me say,
"Guess what happened?" or "Guess what I saw today!"
That makes me happy.

Thank You.

Draw Your Prayer

J

God, Thank You for Junk.

The Bible says...

"Christ himself is the Creator who made everything in heaven and earth, the things we can see and the things we can't; the spirit world with its kings and kingdoms, its rulers and authorities; all were made by Christ for his own use and glory."
Colossians 1:16

Thank you, God, that you understand why I collect "junk" like rocks, whistles, and broken stuff. I like to keep them in my pocket. Then I take them out when I'm sad and they make me think of you. You don't think anything or anyone is "junk."

Thank You.

Draw Your Prayer

K

GOD, THANK YOU FOR MAKING ME A KEEPER.

The Bible says...

"You saw me before I was born and scheduled each day
of my life before I began to breathe. Every day was
recorded in your book!"
Psalm 139:16

In my head God, I sometimes hear you say that I'm a
"keeper." Thank you for that. Especially in the times
when I feel more like a loser. Thank you for keeping me.

Thank You.

Draw Your Prayer

L

GOD, THANK YOU FOR YOUR LOVE.

The Bible says...

"God showed his great love for us by sending Christ to
die for us while we were still sinners."
Romans 5:8

I'm not sure exactly what love is, but thank you God, that
when I think about you and talk to you about my stuff
and my feelings, I feel safe. I think that's what love is.
Feeling safe to just be me with you.

Thank You.

Draw Your Prayer

M

GOD, THANK YOU FOR **MY MIND**.

The Bible says…

"This is the way we know that we belong to the way of truth. When our hearts make us feel guilty, we can still have peace before God. God is greater than our hearts, and he knows everything."
1 John 3:20, ICB

God, why does my mind think mean thoughts sometimes? You never think mean thoughts, do you? I want to grow up to be like you. Thank you for showing me how when I ask.

Thank You.

Draw Your Prayer

N

God, Thank You That You Are Never Too Busy For Me.

The Bible says…

"I will answer them before they even call to me. While they are still talking to me about their needs, I will go ahead and answer their prayers!"
Isaiah 65:24

It doesn't matter what time of the day or night that I talk to you, God, you are never too busy to listen to me.

Thank You.

Draw Your Prayer

GOD, THANK YOU FOR BEING OPEN.

The Bible says...

"Ask and it will be given to you. Search and you will find. Knock and the door will be opened for you. The one who asks will always receive; the one who is searching will always find, and the door is opened to the man who knocks."
Matthew 7:7-8, Phillips

You say the door is always open for me to come in and ask you to be my personal savior. I know I've been bad and I know I can't be good on my own. I need your help. I know you were treated bad and died for everybody.

Thank You.

Draw Your Prayer

P

God, Thank You For Patience.

The Bible says…

"The Lord is not slow in doing what he promised—the
way some people understand slowness. But God is being
patient with you. He does not want anyone to be lost. He
wants everyone to change his heart and life."
2 Peter 3:9, ICB

Ugh! Why did you think up that idea? I don't think I'm very
good at waiting for things. Is it easier for grown-ups? It's
a big word and it's hard to be patient. Prayer is the
answer. Will you help me please?

Thank You.

Draw Your Prayer

Q

God, Thank You For the Quiet.

The Bible says...

"God says, "Be still and know that I am God.
I will be praised in all the nations.
I will be praised throughout the earth."
Psalm 46:10, ICB

When I get real quiet and listen real carefully, I can almost hear your voice telling me really smart things to do.

Thank You.

Draw Your Prayer

R

God, Thank You That I can Run.

The Bible says…

"…we, too, should run the race that is before us and never quit. We should remove from our lives anything that would slow us down and the sin that so often makes us fall."
Hebrews 12:1, ERV

God, I love to run, but I'm learning not to run inside. Sometimes I forget and something gets broken, then I get into trouble. And I promise not to do it again, but then I forget. I wish I would always remember. I want to always run to you.

Thank You.

Draw Your Prayer

God, Thank You For Being My Savior.

The Bible says...

"For God loved the world so much that he gave his only Son so that anyone who believes in him shall not perish but have eternal life."
John 3:16

I'm sure glad you're stronger and smarter than Satan. I used to be afraid of him, until I received Jesus as my savior. Now I know he's with me always.

Thank You.

Draw Your Prayer

God, Thank You That I Can Always Talk to You.

The Bible says...

"In my distress I screamed to the Lord for his help. And he heard me from heaven; my cry reached his ears.
Psalm 18:6

Some of my friends are taller than I am. They laugh at me for being short and it hurts. But it's nothing like how much you hurt when you hung on the cross and died. They called you names, too. Were you short, too, Jesus? Thank you that I can always talk to you about anything.

Thank You.

Draw Your Prayer

U

My Father, Thank You That You Are Unwavering.

The Bible says…

"Jesus Christ is the same yesterday, today, and forever."
Hebrews 13:8

Others may have a love that is conditional and fragile, but I know that You are dependable and unwavering with Your love, always intently pursuing until Your children become Your bride.

Thank You.

Draw Your Prayer

V

My Father, Thank You That You Are the Victor.

The Bible says…

"But we thank God who gives us the victory through our
Lord Jesus Christ!"
1 Corinthians 15:57, ERV

Satan wanted to keep me from You, my Father, but You
are Victor over Satan. Although he wins a few
skirmishes,
You have already won the war.

Thank You.

Draw Your Prayer

W

My Father, Thank You That You Want Time With Me.

The Bible says…

"I am the vine, and you are the branches. If you stay joined to me, and I to you, you will produce plenty of fruit. But separated from me you won't be able to do anything"
John 15:5, ERV

Sometimes it is hard to comprehend that You want time with me – and that I don't have to do anything special to earn Your attention. That makes me feel very good, my Father.

Thank You.

Draw Your Prayer

My Father, Thank You That You Are "X"-tatic.

Your Word says…

"And you will seek Me and find Me,
when you search for Me with all your heart."
Jeremiah 29:13

That is really awesome, my Father – that You are ecstatic
when I seek You and desire to spend time with You. It is hard to understand why someone as important as You would delight to spend time with me, and yet it is true!

Thank You.

Draw Your Prayer

Y

My Father, Thank You That You Yearn For Me.

The Bible says...

"The Spirit that God made to live in us wants us for himself alone."
James 4:5, ICB

The more I spend time in the Scriptures, reading how You relate to Your people, the more I see that You do indeed yearn for me, Your bride, in deep relationship.

Thank You.

Draw Your Prayer

Z

My Father, Thank You That You Are Zealous.

The Bible says...

"Lord, show them your strong love for your people.:
Isaiah 26:11, ICB

Earnest, enthusiastic and eager, You are zealous in Your love for me, Your bride. You shower me with blessings daily. Make me ever mindful of You and zealous in my love for You in return.

Thank You.

Draw Your Prayer

Got a Minute?

If this devotional has impacted your life,
please take a moment to let someone know.
Here are a few ways you can show your support:

Write a book review.

Share or mention *My Father* on social media.
Be sure to use the hashtag #MyFatherAcrosticDevo.

Recommend this book to your friends, family,
Bible study sisters or brothers, church family, or anyone
else you think might enjoy it as much as you have.

Connect with Pam online by visiting
LoavesandFishesCoaching.com.

About The Author

Pam Taylor is passionately in love with Jesus Christ and delights in walking with Him daily. Her greatest joy has been providing for and raising her two adult children. As a result of being a single, homeschooling mom and former missionary to third world countries, Pam discovered her gifts for teaching, discipling, and writing. She is now a Christian Life Coach and Living Your Strengths Mentor.

You can learn more about Pam and connect with her online at LoavesandFishesCoaching.com

Also Available

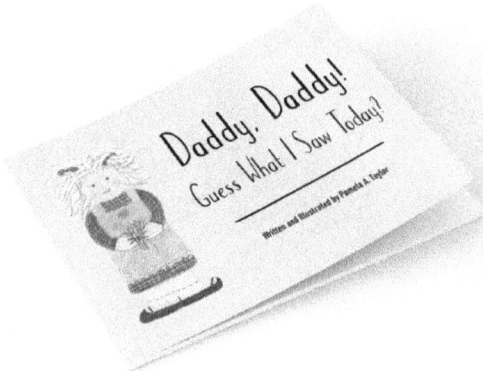

From a flock of geese to a dog on a leash, the pages of this winsome little book are filled with things we see around us every day. Pamela A. Taylor takes those everyday items and looks at them through the eyes of a child; making them seem exciting and new while also teaching children how to be grateful for the God who created them. Take a walk with Pam through the pages of this book and help your little ones see God's hand in the beauty of life.

Daddy Daddy is available wherever books are sold.

www.ingramcontent.com/pod-product-compliance
Lightning Source LLC
Chambersburg PA
CBHW071933020426
42331CB00010B/2849